AF871345

QUOTES FOR INVESTORS

A WEEKLY JOURNAL OF QUOTES FOR PATIENCE, CLARITY AND A SUCCESSFUL INVESTORS MINDSET

THE QUOTIVATION SERIES

DR. JO LUKINS

ELITE

Copyright © 2026 by Dr. Jo Lukins

All rights reserved.

No part of this book may be reproduced in any form or by any electronic or mechanical means, including information storage and retrieval systems, without written permission from the author, except for the use of brief quotations in a book review.

Nothing in this book creates a client or advisory relationship. The content is general in nature and is not tailored to your circumstances. It should not be used as a substitute for professional business, financial, legal, or other advice from a qualified adviser.

ISBN: 978-1-7635127-6-4 (Paperback)

Elite Edge Publishing

www.drjolukins.com

Quotes for Investors invites you to explore wisdom from those who have achieved in business, finance, entertainment, and as thought leaders; thoughtfully selected to support your journey. Set aside time each week to reflect on the quote and consider what it means for you. A diary entry or reminder can help you stay committed.

This journal offers space for your weekly reflections. As you consider each quote, notice which ones resonate and which ones you might question. Both reactions help you better understand your values and approach to performance.

The second part of the book provides further reflection questions. These are designed to give you space for your own thoughts before considering additional prompts.

Looking for some extra accountability to keep you inspired throughout the year?

You can choose to receive a weekly email with each quote and the journal prompts to help you stay motivated and on track. If you'd like to receive a weekly reminder, simply scan the QR code below and you'll start getting an email with the latest quote to help you move closer to your goals.

The quotes are organised into five key areas of successful investing. If you have a particular area you'd like to focus on, use the guide below to find relevant quotes.

WEALTH, FREEDOM AND GROWTH:
Quotes 1, 2, 8, 9, 10, 11, 14, 15, 47, 50, 52

MINDSET AND TEMPERAMENT:
Quotes 3, 4, 5, 6, 16, 17, 33, 46, 49, 51

RISK AND MARKET REALITIES:
Quotes 13, 18, 19, 20, 21, 22, 23, 24, 31, 34

TIME AND PATIENCE:
Quotes 7, 25, 26, 27, 28, 29, 30, 32, 37, 45

STRATEGY, SELECTION AND DIVERSIFICATION:
Quotes 12, 35, 36, 38, 39, 40, 41, 42, 43, 44, 48

Reflect and Perform

Each page offers a quote to spark reflection about your Investing mindset, routines, and team dynamics. Take your time, revisit the quote over a week, and observe how your views might change with ongoing experience.

Some quotes may be familiar, but their true value comes from thoughtful reflection. Consider how you might apply their message to make a lasting difference in your journey.

Performance-Driven Prompts

- After reflecting, what actions or habits could you apply this week in your Investing?
- If a quote feels at odds with your experience, notice what you believe instead, and make notes of your wisdom.

In the final section, you'll find space to add quotes you discover throughout the year, allowing your motivation to grow with you.

I look forward to sharing this journey. Reach out to let me know which quotes inspire you, and the impact they have on your performance and mindset. Shine bright, Dr. Jo (excel@drjolukins.com)

Custom copies for your business, team or organisation. If you'd like your own set of the Quotivation Series, please contact us about creating a custom edition.

ONE

“

Money is a terrible master but an excellent servant

P. T. BARNUM

SHOWMAN AND ENTREPRENEUR WHO BUILT A VAST ENTERTAINMENT EMPIRE

TWO

> I will tell you how to become rich. Be fearful when others are greedy. Be greedy when others are fearful.

WARREN BUFFET

INFLUENTIAL MARKET THINKER;
STEWARD OF BERKSHIRE HATHAWAY

THREE

> "Investing should be more like watching paint dry or watching grass grow. If you want excitement, take money and go to a casino.

PAUL SAMUELSON

NOBEL-WINNING ECONOMIST WHO CHAMPIONED RATIONAL, LOW-COST INVESTING

FOUR

The four most dangerous words in investing are: "This time it's different."

JOHN TEMPLETON

GLOBAL INVESTING PIONEER FAMOUS FOR CONTRARIAN VALUE THINKING

FIVE

> The best investment you can make is in yourself.
>
> **WARREN BUFFETT**
>
> BERKSHIRE HATHAWAY CHAIRMAN; LEGENDARY LONG-TERM INVESTOR.

SIX

> An investment in knowledge pays the best interest.

BENJAMIN FRANKLIN

FOUNDING FATHER, INVENTOR AND WRITER
CELEBRATED FOR PRACTICAL WISDOM

SEVEN

> Spend each day trying to be a little wiser than you were when you woke up.
>
> **CHARLIE MUNGER**
>
> BERKSHIRE VICE CHAIRMAN FAMED FOR JUDGMENT AND MULTIDISCIPLINARY THINKING

EIGHT

“

It’s not your salary that makes you rich, it’s your spending habits

CHARLES A. JAFFE

FINANCIAL JOURNALIST KNOWN FOR PRACTICAL PERSONAL FINANCE GUIDANCE

NINE

> Financial peace isn't the acquisition of stuff. It's learning to live on less than you make.
>
> **DAVE RAMSEY**
>
> DEBT-FREE LIVING ADVOCATE AND WIDELY FOLLOWED MONEY BROADCASTER

TEN

“

Risk comes from not knowing what you’re doing.

WARREN BUFFETT

ONE OF HISTORY'S MOST SUCCESSFUL INVESTORS AND BUSINESS LEADERS

ELEVEN

> “Accept that investing risk can’t be eliminated, but it can be managed.

TRACY Z

DAVE RAMSEY

FINANCE WRITER FOCUSED ON INVESTMENT ADVICE FOR FEMALE ENTREPRENEURS

TWELVE

"The desire to get rich fast is pretty dangerous.

CHARLIE MUNGER

BERKSHIRE VICE CHAIRMAN FAMED FOR JUDGMENT AND MULTIDISCIPLINARY THINKING

THIRTEEN

"

Courage taught me no matter how bad a crisis gets, any sound investment will eventually pay off.

CARLOS SLIM

BILLIONAIRE ENTREPRENEUR AND INVESTOR BEHIND A VAST BUSINESS EMPIRE

FOURTEEN

"

Investing is simple, but not easy.

WARREN BUFFET

AN INVESTOR REVERED FOR HIS WISDOM AND SUCCESS.

FIFTEEN

“

Diversification is protection against ignorance.

WARREN BUFFET

AN INVESTOR REVERED FOR HIS WISDOM AND SUCCESS.

SIXTEEN

> To achieve satisfactory investment results is easier than most people realize; to achieve superior results is harder than it looks.

BENJAMIN GRAHAM

FATHER OF VALUE INVESTING AND MENTOR TO GENERATIONS OF INVESTORS

SEVENTEEN

> "If you don't find a way to make money while you sleep, you will work until you die.

WARREN BUFFETT

FAMED CONTRARIAN INVESTOR WITH UNMATCHED CAPITAL ALLOCATION SKILL

EIGHTEEN

> If you think taking care of yourself is selfish, change your mind.

ANN RICHARDS

FORMER TEXAS GOVERNOR KNOWN FOR CANDID LEADERSHIP AND RESILIENCE

NINETEEN

> "Creating wealth hinges on discipline.

MARIA VANASKI

FINANCIAL ADVISER FOCUSED ON DISCIPLINED WEALTH-BUILDING HABITS

TWENTY

“

The difference between successful people and unsuccessful people is extraordinary determination.

MARY KAY ASH

MARY KAY FOUNDER AND SYMBOL OF DETERMINED ENTREPRENEURSHIP

TWENTY-ONE

"A big part of financial freedom is having your heart and mind free from worry about the what-if's of life."

SUZE ORMAN

BESTSELLING PERSONAL-FINANCE BROADCASTER EMPOWERING PEOPLE TOWARD SECURITY AND CONFIDENCE

TWENTY-TWO

"Financial independence is about more than money; it's about the power to choose.

CARRIE SCHWAB-POMERANTZ

SCHWAB EXECUTIVE CHAMPIONING ACCESSIBLE INVESTOR EDUCATION

TWENTY-THREE

"The most important quality for an investor is temperament, not intellect.

WARREN BUFFETT

ICONIC VALUE INVESTOR WITH EXCEPTIONAL LONG-TERM BUSINESS JUDGMENT

TWENTY-FOUR

“

Investing isn’t about beating others at their game. It’s about controlling yourself at your own game.

BENJAMIN GRAHAM

FATHER OF VALUE INVESTING AND MENTOR TO GENERATIONS OF INVESTORS

TWENTY-FIVE

> “Markets can remain irrational longer than you can remain solvent.

JOHN MAYNARD KEYNES

ECONOMIST WHOSE IDEAS RESHAPED MODERN MACROECONOMICS AND MARKETS

TWENTY-SIX

"The stock market is human nature and crowd psychology on daily display.

HOWARD MARKS

OAKTREE CO-FOUNDER RECOGNISED
FOR MEMOS ON RISK AND CYCLES

TWENTY-SEVEN

"The big money is not in the buying and selling, but in the waiting.

CHARLIE MUNGER

BERKSHIRE VICE CHAIRMAN FAMED FOR JUDGMENT AND MULTIDISCIPLINARY THINKING

TWENTY-EIGHT

> “Price is what you pay. Value is what you get.

WARREN BUFFETT

BILLIONAIRE INVESTOR PRIZED FOR CLARITY, RESTRAINT AND DISCIPLINE.

TWENTY-NINE

“

Behind every stock is a company. Find out what it’s doing.

PETER LYNCH

FAMED FIDELITY MANAGER KNOWN FOR PRACTICAL, BUSINESS-FIRST INVESTING

THIRTY

"Investing without research is like playing stud poker and never looking at the cards.

PETER LYNCH

FAMED FIDELITY MANAGER KNOWN FOR PRACTICAL, BUSINESS-FIRST INVESTING

THIRTY-ONE

“

The goal of the non-professional should not be to pick winners but to own a cross section of businesses that in aggregate are bound to do well.

WARREN BUFFETT

BERKSHIRE HATHAWAY CHAIRMAN; LEGENDARY LONG-TERM INVESTOR

THIRTY-TWO

"

Don't look for the needle in the haystack. Just buy the haystack.

JOHN BOGLE

VANGUARD FOUNDER WHO PIONEERED LOW-COST INDEX FUND INVESTING

THIRTY-THREE

"The first rule of investment is don't lose. The second rule is don't forget the first rule.

WARREN BUFFETT

VETERAN INVESTOR FAMED FOR BUYING QUALITY BUSINESSES LONG TERM

THIRTY-FOUR

“

Time in the market beats timing the market.

KEN FISHER

INVESTMENT MANAGER AND AUTHOR ADVOCATING LONG-TERM MARKET PARTICIPATION

THIRTY-FIVE

“The best time to plant a tree was 20 years ago. The second-best time is now.

CHINESE PROVERB

THIRTY-SIX

> Know what you own and know why you own it.

PETER LYNCH

FAMED FIDELITY MANAGER KNOWN FOR PRACTICAL, BUSINESS-FIRST INVESTING

THIRTY-SEVEN

"Your net worth to the world is usually determined by what remains after your bad habits are subtracted from your good ones.

BENJAMIN FRANKLIN

FOUNDING FATHER, INVENTOR AND WRITER CELEBRATED FOR PRACTICAL WISDOM

THIRTY-EIGHT

“

If you’re not making mistakes, then you’re not making decisions.

CATHERINE COOK

ENTREPRENEUR ADVOCATING LEARNING THROUGH ACTION AND EXPERIMENTATION

THIRTY-NINE

"To be an investor you must be a believer in a better tomorrow.

BENJAMIN GRAHAM

FATHER OF VALUE INVESTING AND MENTOR TO GENERATIONS OF INVESTORS

FORTY

> Wealth consists not in having great possessions, but in having few wants.

EPICTETUS

STOIC PHILOSOPHER WHOSE TEACHINGS CHAMPIONED DISCIPLINE AND INNER FREEDOM

FORTY-ONE

“Spend less than you earn; invest the surplus; avoid debt, and you will succeed.

WILLIAM J. BERNSTEIN

FINANCIAL THEORIST AND AUTHOR ON ASSET ALLOCATION, HISTORY AND LONG-TERM INVESTING

FORTY-TWO

"Every time you borrow money, you're robbing your future self.

NATHAN W. MORRIS

WRITER WHOSE REFLECTIONS FOCUS ON DEBT AND PERSONAL DISCIPLINE

FORTY-THREE

"

Compound interest is the eighth wonder of the world. He who understands it, earns it; he who doesn't, pays it.

ALBERT EINSTEIN

WORLD-RENOWNED PHYSICIST OFTEN CITED ON COMPOUNDING AND LONG-TERM THINKING

FORTY-FOUR

> Money is made by sitting, not trading.

JESSE LIVERMORE

LEGENDARY TRADER REMEMBERED FOR LESSONS ON SPECULATION AND PATIENCE

FORTY-FIVE

> It's far better to buy a wonderful company at a fair price than a fair company at a wonderful price.

WARREN BUFFETT

LEGENDARY STOCK PICKER WHOSE PRINCIPLES SHAPED MODERN INVESTING

FORTY-SIX

“

The stock market is a no-called-strike game. You don’t have to swing at everything.

WARREN BUFFETT

MASTER CAPITAL ALLOCATOR CELEBRATED FOR PATIENCE, DISCIPLINE AND COMPOUNDING

FORTY-SEVEN

“

I came to financial peace not by getting everything, but by learning to deal well with what I already had.

TERRY SAVAGE

FINANCIAL JOURNALIST KNOWN FOR PRACTICAL MONEY AND PLANNING ADVICE

FORTY-EIGHT

"When it is obvious that the goals cannot be reached, don't adjust the goals, adjust the action steps.

CONFUCIUS

ANCIENT PHILOSOPHER WHOSE TEACHINGS SHAPED ETHICS AND SELF-MASTERY

FORTY-NINE

“

Money is not the goal. Money has no value. The value comes from the dreams money helps achieve.

OPRAH WINFREY

MEDIA LEADER AND PHILANTHROPIST LINKING WEALTH WITH PURPOSE

FIFTY

"It is not necessary to do extraordinary things to get extraordinary results.

WARREN BUFFETT

MASTER CAPITAL ALLOCATOR CELEBRATED FOR PATIENCE AND COMPOUNDING

FIFTY-ONE

“

When you invest, you are purchasing a day when you won’t have to work.

AYA LARAYA

FINANCIAL WRITER FOCUSED ON INVESTING FOR FUTURE FREEDOM

FIFTY-TWO

"The poor and the middle class work for money. The rich have money work for them.

ROBERT KIYOSAKI

AUTHOR OF RICH DAD POOR DAD AND FINANCIAL-EDUCATION ENTREPRENEUR

“You’ll find my reflection questions in the following section. They’ve been included separately so you can first explore your own ideas and see what stands out to you.

This is your opportunity to stretch your thinking, challenge your habits, and connect each concept to your training and performance in a real and personal way.

Once you’ve completed your initial reflections, take a moment to read through the additional questions. See what sparks your curiosity or pushes you to think differently. Go back to your earlier notes and build on them; this is where real growth happens.

This process is designed to help you get the most from your reflections and keep your focus on progress, not perfection. Your effort in this space will be reflected in how you show up in your leadership and your life.

DR. JO

ONE

> Money is a terrible master but an excellent servant.
>
> P. T. BARNUM

When money controls your choices, life feels cramped; when you control money, it becomes a tool for your values.

- Where does money currently control you?
- If your spending reflected your deepest values, what would change first?
- What simple step would move you from reacting to money to giving it clear directions?

TWO

> I will tell you how to become rich. Be fearful when others are greedy. Be greedy when others are fearful
>
> WARREN BUFFET

Crowds often rush in at the top and run away at the bottom. Going against extreme enthusiasm or panic, with careful thinking, can create powerful opportunities.

- What topic, if you understood it better, would immediately improve your decisions?
- How can you turn a small part of each day into learning?
- When has learning saved you time, money, or regret?

THREE

> Investing should be more like watching paint dry or watching grass grow. If you want excitement, take money and go to a casino.
>
> PAUL SAMUELSON

Steady, uneventful investing is usually a good sign. Chasing thrills with money tends to feel exciting now and painful later.

- Where are you looking for excitement with your money?
- How would your investing change if you accepted that patience is a feature?
- What place in your life could you seek excitement instead of in your portfolio?

FOUR

> The four most dangerous words in investing are: *This time it's different.*
>
> JOHN TEMPLETON

Human behavior tends to repeat itself. Forgetting history can lead you to take risks that look new but are actually very old mistakes.

- Where are you tempted to believe the rules no longer apply to you?
- What past market lessons are you at risk of ignoring?
- How can you consider history before making decisions?

FIVE

> The best investment you can make is in yourself.
>
> WARREN BUFFET

Skills, character and health are assets that you control. Before chasing external opportunities, strengthen who you are and what you can do.

- Where in your life are you relying on luck instead of building your own capability?
- What is one skill you could start developing this week that your future self would thank you for?
- If your growth were a portfolio, which area of you is most underinvested right now?

SIX

> An investment in knowledge pays the best interest.
>
> BENJAMIN FRANKLIN

Learning compounds over time, improving every decision you make.

- What topic, if you understood it better, would immediately improve your decisions?
- How can you turn a small part of each day into learning time?
- When did learning something once save you time, money, or regret later?

SEVEN

> Spend each day trying to be a little wiser than you were when you woke up.
>
> CHARLIE MUNGER

Wisdom is about repeated small insights and better choices over time.

- What did today teach you that you didn't know yesterday?
- If you repeated today every day for a year, would you become wiser or just older?
- What tiny daily habit could nudge you toward wisdom and wealth?

EIGHT

> It's not your salary that makes you rich, it's your spending habits.
>
> CHARLES A. JAFFE

A high income cannot outrun poor habits.

- Which spending habit silently drains the most from your future?
- If someone saw your bank statement, what would they say your priorities are?
- What one habit change could free up the most money for saving or investing this year?

NINE

> Financial peace isn't the acquisition of stuff. It's learning to live on less than you make.
>
> DAVE RAMSAY

Living below your means creates breathing room, choices, and freedom from constant worry.

- Where have you confused more things with more security?
- What small adjustment could create a little more space between what you earn and what you spend?
- If you already owned enough, how would your financial behavior change this month?

TEN

> Risk comes from not knowing what you're doing.
>
> WARREN BUFFETT

Uncertainty feels most dangerous when you have not taken time to understand. Knowledge does not remove risk, but it helps you see it.

- Which area of your finances currently feels confusing?
- What is one step you could take this week to improve your understanding?
- How often are you saying yes to things you don't understand?

ELEVEN

> Accept that investing risk can't be eliminated - but it can be managed
>
> TRACY Z

Some uncertainty is the price of progress and growth. The goal is not to avoid all risk, but to choose risks carefully and protect yourself.

- Where in your life are you paralysed due to risk?
- What risks are you already taking without admitting it to yourself?
- How could you structure your next big decision so the worst-case scenario is bearable?

TWELVE

> The desire to get rich fast is pretty dangerous.
>
> CHARLIE MUNGER

Wanting quick wealth often pushes you toward risky schemes, overconfidence and choices you may not understand. Prosperity usually comes from patience, learning and steady effort over time.

- Where are you hoping for shortcuts?
- What has *quick money* cost you in stress, trust or time?
- If you took a 10-year view of your finances, what would you do differently today?

THIRTEEN

> Courage taught me no matter how bad a crisis gets, any sound investment will eventually pay off.
>
> CARLOS SLIM

Good decisions can look wrong when everything around you feels turbulent. With patience, sound choices often prove themselves.

- Which of your decisions needs patience over panic?
- How do you tell the difference between a sound choice and a reckless one?
- What helps you be courageous when headlines are loud?

FOURTEEN

> Investing is simple, but not easy.
>
> WARREN BUFFETT

The core principles to spend less, invest wisely, be patient are straightforward, but sticking to them under pressure is hard.

- Where do you already know what to do but struggle to follow through?
- When do emotions most often pull you away from simple, sensible actions?
- What small routine could automate the *challenging* parts for you?

FIFTEEN

> Diversification is protection against ignorance.
>
> WARREN BUFFET

There's a broad scope of opportunity in investing. The diversification advantage is protecting against what we do not know or anticipate.

- How diverse is your portfolio and spread of your risk?
- How do you broaden your knowledge in the areas of your investments?
- What questions do you ask of yourself and others to address any gaps in your knowledge?

SIXTEEN

> To achieve satisfactory investment results is easier than most people realize; to achieve superior results is harder than it looks.
>
> BENJAMIN GRAHAM

Doing well over time is achievable with wise habits. Trying to *beat* everyone else, however, is difficult and lead you into unnecessary risk.

- Is your goal to be secure in your gains, or to *win* against others?
- Where has reaching for superior results kept you awake at night?
- What would an *enough* outcome look like for you?

SEVENTEEN

> If you don't find a way to make money while you sleep, you will work until you die.
>
> WARREN BUFFETT

Relying only on active work means your income stops when you do. Building assets that earn on your behalf gives you options later in life.

- What % of your income comes from assets, not hours?
- What small step could you take this year toward income that does not depend on your daily effort?
- If you had more sleep-while-you-earn income, how would that change your choices about work and time?

EIGHTEEN

> If you think taking care of yourself is selfish, change your mind.
>
> ANN RICHARDS

Looking after your body, mind and finances enables you to contribute more, not less. Neglecting yourself limits how you show up for others.

- Where are you running on empty?
- What form of rest, support or planning would make you stronger for others?
- How would your life change if you treated self-care as a responsibility, not a luxury?

NINETEEN

> Creating wealth hinges on discipline.
>
> MARIA VANASKI

Wealth is built more by consistent behaviors than by one-off windfalls. Discipline in spending and saving lets time and compounding do the heavy lifting.

- Which of your goals need a trade-off decision?
- What habit or comfort must you release to move forward?
- What is the price for getting what you want?

TWENTY

> The difference between successful people and unsuccessful people is extraordinary determination.
>
> MARY KAY ASH

Progress usually belongs to the person who keeps going when others stop.

- Where in your life have you given up too soon?
- If you truly believed determination beats talent, what would you start again?
- How can you make it easier to persist on hard days; who or what could support you?

TWENTY-ONE

> A big part of financial freedom is having your heart and mind free from worry about the what-ifs of life.
>
> SUZE ORMAN

Money is not just about numbers, but about how calm or anxious you feel when you think about the future.

- What money worry pops into your mind most often?
- Which simple protection (a small emergency fund, insurance, or a plan) would reduce that anxiety the most?
- How would you behave differently with money if you felt genuinely safe, not scared?

TWENTY-TWO

> Financial independence is about more than money; it's about the power to choose.
>
> CARRIE SCHWAB-POMERANTZ

Independence means having enough stability and resources that you can say yes or no from a place of freedom, not fear.

- Where in your life do you currently feel the money trap?
- If you had more financial flexibility, what is the first thing you would choose differently?
- What step today could slightly increase your power to choose in the future?

TWENTY-THREE

> The most important quality for an investor is temperament, not intellect.
>
> WARREN BUFFET

Good temperament and calmness keeps you from making emotional decisions when markets or life feel chaotic.

- When did emotion last hijack a money/career decision?
- What helps you stay steady when others are panicking?
- How could you design rules for yourself so you rely less on mood and more on wisdom?

TWENTY-FOUR

> Investing isn't about beating others at their game. It's about controlling yourself at your own game.
>
> BENJAMIN GRAHAM

Success comes from a plan that fits your goals and risk tolerance. The contest is between long-term intentions and short-term impulses.

- In what areas of life are you secretly competing with others instead of staying true to your path?
- What would your money decisions look like if you stopped comparing?
- Where do you most need more self-control rather than more information?

TWENTY-FIVE

> Markets can remain irrational longer than you can remain solvent.
>
> JOHN MAYNARD KEYNES

Prices can behave wildly for longer than patience, cash or nerves can last. Betting that markets will *come to their senses* can be costly.

- How exposed are you if a situation stays irrational for much longer than you expect?
- What could you change so that you can survive being *right* later than you hoped?

TWENTY-SIX

> The stock market is human nature and crowd psychology on daily display.
>
> HOWARD MARKS

Markets are made of fear, hope and greed. Understanding people gives insight to price swings, decisions and behaviors.

- Which of your emotions most often interferes with wise financial choices?
- How does your behavior change when you see others winning or losing money quickly?
- What could you do to observe your reactions before you act on them?

TWENTY-SEVEN

> The big money is not in the buying and selling, but in the waiting.
>
> CHARLIE MUNGER

Significant gains often come from holding quality decisions long enough for their benefits to unfold.

- Which of your good decisions needs more time, not more tinkering?
- When have you cut short a promising path because results were not fast enough?
- How can you remind yourself the value of patience?

TWENTY-EIGHT

> Price is what you pay. Value is what you get.
>
> WARREN BUFFETT

The cost of something and its true worth are not the same. Wise decisions look beyond price tags to long-term benefits and quality.

- Where in your life have you prioritised something that was cheap but not valuable?
- What purchases or investments have been expensive yet deeply worthwhile?
- How could you train yourself to ask *What value do I really get?* before you spend?

TWENTY-NINE

> Behind every stock is a company. Find out what it's doing.
>
> PETER LYNCH

A share is not just a symbol; it is a slice of a business serving people. Remembering this helps you think like an owner, not a gambler.

- Do you consider your investments as businesses?
- What do you want to know about a company before trusting it with your money?
- How does business-partner-thinking influence decisions?

THIRTY

> Investing without research is like playing stud poker and never looking at the cards.
>
> PETER LYNCH

Putting money into something you haven't studied is more gambling than investing. Research can save you from big, avoidable mistakes.

- Where are you currently *playing* with money without really looking at the cards?
- What simple research step could you add before any new financial commitment?
- How might your results change if you paused to investigate instead of guessing?

THIRTY-ONE

> The goal of the non-professional should not be to pick winners but to own a cross section of businesses that in aggregate are bound to do well.
>
> WARREN BUFFETT

Trying to find a winner is hard; owning a broad mix of good businesses is more realistic. Diversification lets you benefit from overall progress without needing to predict every champion.

- Where in your financial life are you putting too much pressure?
- How could you build healthy diversification?

THIRTY-TWO

> Don't look for the needle in the haystack. Just buy the haystack.
>
> JOHN BOGLE

Instead of searching for rare, elusive winners, you can consider broader funds. This approach offers simplicity and diversification.

- How much energy are you spending trying to find needles instead of owning haystacks?
- What appeals to you about simplicity, and what scares you about it?

THIRTY-THREE

> The first rule of investment is don't lose. The second rule is don't forget the first rule.
>
> WARREN BUFFETT

Protecting your capital is the foundation for growing it. Avoiding big, permanent losses often matters more than chasing spectacular gains.

- Where are you risking a large loss for a small gain?
- If you applied *don't lose first* to your time and energy, what would you stop doing?
- What boundaries would protect your base?

THIRTY-FOUR

> Time in the market beats timing the market.
>
> KEN FISHER

Staying invested through ups and downs usually beats trying to jump in and out with precision. Patience and consistency often outperform clever guesses about short-term moves.

- Where are you waiting for the perfect moment instead of taking a sensible step now?
- How many good opportunities have you missed by trying to predict instead of participate?
- What would it mean for you to commit to a long-term plan and simply stick to it?

THIRTY-FIVE

> The best time to plant a tree was 20 years ago. The second-best time is now. Chinese proverb
>
> CHINESE PROVERB

Regret about not starting earlier can keep you from starting at all. The sooner you begin the sooner time starts working in your favour.

- Where are you using *too late* as an excuse to stay still?
- If you planted one *tree* in your finances, health or learning today, what would it be?
- How can you turn previous regret into energy for now?

THIRTY-SIX

> Know what you own and know why you own it.
>
> PETER LYNCH

Clarity about your assets and your reasons for holding them creates confidence and better decisions. Owning things you don't understand sets you up for fear and impulsive reactions.

- If you listed everything you own financially, where would your understanding be weakest?
- Why do you hold each major investment. Could you explain it in one sentence?
- What is one holding you might need to study more?

THIRTY-SEVEN

> Your net worth to the world is usually determined by what remains after your bad habits are subtracted from your good ones.
>
> BENJAMIN FRANKLIN

Who you are is shaped by your strengths and self-sabotage. Reducing harmful habits can lift your life faster than adding new ones.

- Which habit quietly subtracts from your potential?
- What existing good habit deserves more support and attention from you?
- If you removed one bad habit this year, how would your impact on others change?

THIRTY-EIGHT

> If you're not making mistakes, then you're not making decisions.
>
> CATHERINE COOK

Errors are an unavoidable part of an active, learning life. Avoiding all mistakes often means avoiding growth, responsibility and courage.

- Where are you so afraid of mistakes that you stay stuck?
- What recent mistake taught you something useful?
- How could you build a habit of reviewing your errors kindly and wisely?

THIRTY-NINE

> To be an investor you must be a believer in a better tomorrow.
>
> BENJAMIN GRAHAM

Optimism in tomorrow helps you stay committed when today feels negative.

- What does a better tomorrow look like for you?
- If optimistic about the future, how does that change your money decisions today?
- Where are fear or pessimism causing you to be passive about financial decisions?

FORTY

> Wealth consists not in having great possessions, but in having few wants.
>
> EPICTETUS

True wealth is as much about inner contentment as outer abundance.

- What are you chasing that, if you were honest, does not truly matter to you?
- If you needed less to feel satisfied, what freedom would that create in your life?
- Which wants are actually other people's expectations rather than your own values?

FORTY-ONE

> Spend less than you earn; invest the surplus; avoid debt and you will succeed.
>
> WILLIAM J. BERNSTEIN

The challenge is not complexity, but sticking with the basics when shortcuts look tempting.

- Which of these behaviors is could you improve?
- What is one realistic change you can make this week?
- If you fully lived these three principles for the next decade, how different might your life look?

FORTY-TWO

> Every time you borrow money, you're robbing your future self.
>
> NATHAN W. MORRIS

Debt trades tomorrow's freedom for today's comfort. Seeing borrowing this way makes every loan a question about how you want to treat your future self.

- If your future self could speak to you today, what would they say about your finances?
- Which current expenses are tomorrow's obligations dressed up as treats?

FORTY-THREE

> Compound interest is the eighth wonder of the world. He who understands it, earns it; he who doesn't, pays it.
>
> ALBERT EINSTEIN

Small amounts, growing over long periods, can turn into large sums; either as savings or as debt. Your choices decide.

- Which part of your life currently benefits from compounding, and which suffers from it?
- If you kept one positive habit for 10 years, what be?
- What debt/habit is quietly working against you now?

FORTY-FOUR

> Money is made by sitting, not trading.
>
> JESSE LIVERMORE

Constant activity is not the same as progress. Often, choosing well and then being patient beats endless tinkering and reacting.

- Where are you confusing busyness with effectiveness in your life or finances?
- What good decisions have you second-guessing, and why?
- How could you create conditions that make it easier to wait calmly on good choices?

FORTY-FIVE

> It's far better to buy a wonderful company at a fair price than a fair company at a wonderful price.
>
> WARREN BUFFETT

Quality tends to reward you more over time than bargains. Paying sensibly for excellence often beats chasing things that are *cheap*.

- Where are you settling for *fair* when you could patiently wait for *wonderful*?
- What in your life has proven that quality, though not cheapest, was worth it?
- How might this idea apply across your choices?

FORTY-SIX

> The stock market is a no-called-strike game. You don't have to swing at everything.
>
> WARREN BUFFETT

You are not forced to act on every opportunity. Waiting for situations you understand and believe in can protect you from mistakes.

- Where do you feel pressure to act quickly?
- What recent "opportunity" might you have been better off ignoring?
- How could you define what a truly good pitch looks like for you in money and life?

FORTY-SEVEN

> I came to financial peace not by getting everything, but by learning to deal well with what I already had.
>
> TERRY SAVAGE

Contentment grows by managing and appreciating your resources. How you handle *enough* often matters more than chasing *more.*

- Where are you waiting for more before being responsible or grateful?
- How could you treat your current income and assets with more care and appreciation?
- What might help you notice what you already have?

FORTY-EIGHT

> When it is obvious that the goals cannot be reached, don't adjust the goals, adjust the action steps.
>
> CONFUCIUS

Even when your first plan fails, the goal may be right. Rather than shrinking your dreams, you can change strategy, pace or methods.

- Which goal have you quietly lowered instead of changing your approach?
- What is one new action step you have not yet tried?
- How can you separate the worth of your goal from the frustration of your current plan?

FORTY-NINE

> Money is not the goal. Money has no value. The value comes from the dreams money helps achieve.
>
> OPRAH WINFREY

Money is a tool, not a purpose; its real meaning lies in what it allows you to create, give and experience.

- If money was no issue, how would you spend your time?
- Where are you chasing money without a clear focus?
- How could you align your spending more closely with your intentions?

FIFTY

> It is not necessary to do extraordinary things to get extraordinary results.
>
> WARREN BUFFETT

The ordinary behaviors most people overlook are usually what create extraordinary outcomes.

- Where are you chasing dramatic moves instead of strengthening simple habits?
- What small action, done daily for a year, would quietly transform your finances?
- How can you make your preferred behaviors easier to repeat without thinking?

FIFTY-ONE

> When you invest, you are purchasing a day when you won't have to work.
>
> AYA LARAYA

Money you set aside today can buy you freedom of time tomorrow. Each wise investment is like pre-paying for future days of choice.

- How many future days are you currently trading on today's impulses?
- If you saw every investment as buying future time, what would you change?

FIFTY-TWO

> The poor and the middle class work for money. The rich have money work for them.
>
> ROBERT KIYOSAKI

Money spent thoughtlessly earns you nothing further, but money invested becomes a tireless worker that keeps generating income and building wealth long after you've stopped actively earning it.

- Where are you still trading time for money that could work for you instead?
- What's one asset you could start building this year?
- Is your money belief helping or limiting you?

OTHER QUOTES TO INSPIRE

Use this section to collect quotes that inspire you throughout the year. Add a few notes about why each quote stands out or what it means to you personally.

To read more from the Quotivation series

The Quotivation Series is a collection of reflective quote journals designed to take short bites of wisdom, and applying it in a practical way to your upcoming success.

Quotes for Athletes: *A weekly journal of quotes for grit, motivation and a winning mindset.*
Quotes for Coaches: *A weekly journal of quotes for leadership, motivation and excellence.*
Quotes for Referees: *A weekly journal of quotes for focus, poise and resilience.*
Quotes for Business: *A weekly journal of quotes for strategy, growth and success.*
Quotes for Leaders: *A weekly journal of quotes for vision, courage, and inspired achievement.*
Quotes for Investors: *A weekly journal of quotes for patience, clarity and a successful investors mindset.*
Quotes for Military: *A weekly journal of quotes for courage, discipline, and an unbreakable mindset in service.*
Quotes for Parenting: *A weekly journal of quotes for patience, guidance, and love.*
Quotes for Students: *A weekly journal of quotes for focus, persistence and curiosity.*
Quotes for You: *A weekly journal of quotes for growth, self-discovery, and an empowered mindset.*

The Quotivation Series is being released through 2026.
Visit my website **drjolukins.com** to be the first to order your copy or visit your preferred indie bookstore or online platform.

Custom copies for your team or business

If you'd like to share a book from the Quotivation Series with an organisation, team or clients, please contact us to discuss creating a custom edition.

Email us at **excel@drjolukins.com** to find out more.

Read more with Dr. Jo

The following books are available at your favourite book store or online platform:

The Elite: Think like an athlete, succeed like a champion. Ten things the elite do differently. 2019

In the Grandstands: The sporting parents guide to raising a confident and happy teen in the highs and lows of youth sports. 2020

The Game Plan: Your 5-month coaching program to champion high performance habits (High Performance Thinking). 2022

The Elite and The Game Plan 2 in 1 Book: Champion your success with elite habits to unleash your winning potential with 10 proven strategies and high-performance coaching program. 2023

Belief: Building unshakeable confidence. 2024

The Whistle Blower: The mental toughness rulebook for referees, umpires, and sports officials. 2025.

The Whistle Blower Workbook: The mental toughness rulebook for referees, umpires, and sports officials. 2025

A NOTE FROM DR. JO

Referred to as a psychological Indiana Jones, thanks to more than twenty-five years spent exploring what helps people achieve their best. I have enjoyed bringing together these quotes for you. If you'd like to connect or learn more, you can always find me at www.drjolukins.com.

If Quotes for Investors has made an impact for you, I'd be grateful if you would share your thoughts or leave a review on Amazon or Goodreads. Similarly, if you'd like to share your favorite quote with me, let me know at excel@drjolukins.com

Shine Bright, Dr. Jo

www.ingramcontent.com/pod-product-compliance
Lightning Source LLC
LaVergne TN
LVHW051931051126
851857LV00020B/2070
* 9 7 8 1 7 6 4 4 1 3 4 1 1 *